Losing the Moon

Losing the Moon

Poems by

Kathryn Levy

Kathryn Levy

To Margery,
You have a
wonderful daughter.
Congratulations!

Best
Kathryn

Canio's Editions

ACKNOWLEDGMENTS

Grateful acknowledgment is made to the editors of the following journals in which these poems first appeared: *The Manhattan Poetry Review*, "Railroad Crossing"; *Provincetown Arts*, "Air." My thanks to the Wendy Glass Gallery in Manhattan, where the poem "Readings" first appeared.

Cover art: Ramon Alcolea, *Olvido VII*

Cover photograph: Ken Robbins

Author photograph: Joyce Ravid

Designed by The Grenfell Press, New York

I would like to thank Yaddo, the Virginia Center for the Creative Arts, The Ragdale Foundation, the Blue Mountain Center, and Cummington Community for the Arts, where many of these poems were written. Thanks also to the writers and friends who have advised me on several of these poems: Jill Bialosky, Kenny Fries, Karen Krieger, and Patricia Thackray.

I wish to acknowledge Bogdan Kostrzynski, whose painting *Arrival* was a source for the poem "Ledges." And a warm thanks to Rona Kluger, Michelle Audet, and Douglas Newby.

I am very grateful for the editorial advice and support of Canio Pavone.

ISBN 1-886435-16-2

Library of Congress Control Number: 2006900340

Canio's Editions
Distributed by Canio's Books
290 Main Street
Sag Harbor, NY 11963
www.caniosbooks.com

In memory of my father and my godmother

Sidney Levy

and

Evelyn Goldberg

For the missing, nothing is impossible.

—Botho Strauss, *Big/Little*
(tr. Christopher Martin)

Contents

IV. Mating Time

V. Losing the Moon

I

Telling Stories

Telling Stories

A dancer on the roof spun
into her end. We saw her body falling
and a face pressed against the ground.
It can't answer.
Someone says: she must have been angry.
Someone says: she must have been tired
and sad and weak and strong enough
just to end, to stop spinning.
I've had her picture framed.
I keep it near the books I read,
the flowers I buy to make my room
sweet, fresh. We dropped
masses of white all over the grave—
the rain came and tore them away, so slowly.
Her brother calls from miles away:
I miss her, I miss asking questions.
We exchange stories. I speak to her each night
telling a story: Once, I wanted to die,
but didn't. And then the leaves turned in the wind
bright, so new. That can happen.
Her face is always averted.
You can't make the dead listen
as you walk out the door, return and say:
I'll be back in two hours, just
wait for me. You can't know
she's gone already. Did I want to die?
I stayed up all night thinking of death,
then fell to sleep. Was she playing at death?
The brilliant lights glared
from everywhere, hundreds applauded.
It was hard to see. The performance is fast
and always new. Someone broke the tight circle—we all
hurtled.

Hundreds of Nights

Someone is spending a life
up in the attic, preparing.

Last night he whispered,
come to me. I was too far away.

But I dreamed his voice
waiting for mine. In another room

an old woman paces slowly
wanting me to join her

for company—that's all that's left.
At the end of the day a beam cracks

somewhere inside each haunted house.
A child thinks—it's my ghost,

she's coming to get me.
Her grandmother smiles, she knows

too much. It must be his
crucial approach. That's what I thought

hundreds of nights ago.
No ghosts came, no lost friend

with kind hands. I held the air
all night. It was so soft.

So what is left? My hands
are old now, they shake for help.

And preparing is cold,
it reminds me

of too little. But I still can hear.
Listen—that was almost

a sound.

Readings

The birds begun at Four o'clock—
Their period for Dawn—
                    Emily Dickinson

I speak to the birds.
I give them my readings and they
give me theirs.
And the clouds rush by
regardless of us.
And the birds rush by, ignoring
all my stories—I haven't forgotten.
And I haven't forgotten
that they must sing
for some obscure, incessant reason.
One calls to her lover—come closer.
I love to pretend
I'm calling to someone, I'm hearing
every sound that's echoed through
my thin curtains.
As the sounds escape out of me
I whisper—what was that?
Someone might hear.
He's listening outside the door
or a thousand miles away,
as I listen to the foreign birds
each in her own
dear compartment.
How odd it is—
they'll never know
(and they wouldn't care)
they're singing beyond
themselves.

Folded Hands

—I am in danger—Sir—
Emily Dickinson

Those birds that rushed
away from the fields
have been lost for months,
and you still wait
for a shivering wing, the icy
eye of a bird
as it stares, as it passes
much too quickly.
It's been chill for months—
you've kept the windows
tightly shut and haven't emerged
from your tiny room. For five days
you sat near the window
with folded hands and those
glaring eyes. People call
from down below,
how are you today? You say,
I'm walking a wire
—to yourself alone. They're shouting,
how are you today?—I'm walking a wire
that's quiet, suspended
above a crowd of strange faces.
They are waiting for
a clear end, a calm hand to reach
out to them. The hand might shiver,
the wire might shake
in the dancing wind. The audience glares
and the birds rush back—they explode
into the suddenly
brilliant air.
You have to run towards them
—right now—
on the
impossible wire
you take—a step—

Another Year

A woman spreads
through her house: an old
tablecloth, sheets,
a broken dish
mismatched
with another,
and walks across
a bare room,
one hand holding
her shoulder.
She doesn't look up.
It's mourning for nothing
the world would notice:
each second slipping
into nothing,
the face she saw
across from her
that never appeared
completely.
He's completely silent,
as the house might be,
except for the cracks
she soothes in the floor
with her bare feet.
She's worn her nightgown
all day, and her feet
are old. But that
is nothing.—
She only has to look
up and get out

from everywhere.
The clock ticks
far inside
some next room:
it's hard to hear.
And stay calm: it's nothing,
it's nothing.

Indoors

My last excursion into the cold
was too much. I've been staying indoors for weeks,
recalling the blast of wind that slammed
into my face, the treacherous street
with nothing to hold. The street was so dark,
there was no one to see. I stayed beneath
a cracked tree for two minutes thinking,
I'll never be warm, I'll never get home.

Somehow those moments end. The white walls
shelter me, I try to sleep. I try to say,
the wind beating against my glass
will never enter. I've put up blankets
instead of drapes. I never take them down.
There are friends who call with questions:
When will we meet? There's a lover I lost
two months ago. His letters

fill one drawer. They ask:
When will we meet? I've decided
it's better not to meet. The wind pulled me
through the dark. By chance
I made it back. The electric
lights are hard, the room swelters,
but I made it back. Tomorrow,
I'll burn all the letters, I'll stop the phone,

I'll imagine my mail,
and the glittering snow that fills the distant park
so peacefully. No one rips through
so it lasts for months. Somehow each month ends.
I fill the pages of a leather book
with worlds I've known: two minutes under a tree, my last
walk with my lover. Those worlds
are trapped here. It's like a brilliant photograph—

someone stares from the photograph
with a rigid smile.
Her hand is locked in someone's hand,
just out of the picture. It's winter.
It will always be winter. The hand
will keep clutching.
She will have to smile
forever.

Echoes

The buzzer rings so hard
you shake for hours. The message is:
you have a package, you have a friend
coming to visit, we need to repair the walls.
And a day is spent breaking the wall,
or sealing the wall, or painting the cracks
over. This is necessary,
it's not a game. The package comes
from a frightened lover. It's his latest tape—
don't leave me, don't leave
anything. The walls hold leaks,
rats, the whole structure
cracking to pieces—they have to repair.
The friend (he was waiting)
has to talk for just a while,
and then he leaves, you forget the subject, feel
so deserted. The package has been
discarded, the leak is safe,
you started something hours ago,
but it's time to sleep.—Sleep, just sleep
as hard as you can.
You could take the buzzer
out of the wall, and threaten to.
But it's quiet for weeks
as you try to focus on one pause: this is
a closed room
on a quiet block
just off the highway, you can barely hear
the trucks, or feel
their hard echoes. And the drills can't start
until 8 a.m. They stop at 5.
And the buzzer is still
mute,
imbedded—

Enfolded in Home

The walls are trembling
the children
won't stop shouting:
Daddy come out
we need you to be
completely here

he hides
under the desks
behind a pile
of half-read books:
I am trying to study

to find my escape

remember the day
the baby ran
across the lawn
for the first time?
Look—she is running
he felt so free

the father of a bird
a king in a tower
making
hours of magic

she can talk now
she hovers around
the narrow room
talking and talking
his son pounds
a spoon on a plate

and all the fragments
fall to the ground

Daddy keeps holding himself
—no one will notice

it is time to put
the books away
to look in the faces
that stare from the table

What is wrong?

he clutches a knife
I will leave tonight
when all the bodies
are put to sleep

and shudders a little
But this
is my home
enfolded in home
for the rest of these nights

he carves the meat
cuts a slice
in one finger

it bleeds

but oh
so slightly—no one
will notice

The Man by the Lake

I can call the blue
sea of the sky
a dead ocean of air
if that's what you want
and sit beside the flat lake
answering questions:
What went wrong?
the blue glared
through my window
too hard: it blinded me
with no meanings
And why did you need
meanings?
I stayed in bed too long
and tried to rise
and it becomes
harder each year
those colors are strange
I can look in the bright
eye of a child
in a photograph
say—that was me
you can see the sign
already—*And what*
was the sign?
I didn't want anything
—you have to want
a room full of things
or merely one
brilliance: that
name for the sky
which has nothing to do
with the sky
I couldn't stop knowing that
as my hollow ocean engulfed
every thing
you see—
I can still speak of oceans
if that's what you want
is it very beautiful here?
is that what you call it?

The Gift

I had it stuffed
—the bird you caught
by the lake, flying.
The bullet hit
in the right place,
her shudder came
from deep inside,
she trembled as
she fell. Her wings
seemed so frail.
The brilliant red
mark you made
turned brown and caked
all over her.
I had to scrape it
off. Look at the good
job I've done—
the wings seem like
flying, the taut
wires I used
to make her fly
are those tiny bones
that birds must have
if we looked inside.
These white feathers
shine in the dark.
Turn the lights out
and watch. It's an icon.
I worked on it
all winter. Remember?
You asked me to.
It's just like life.
The beak and the eyes
were the hardest part,
but then they came
to life.
They're frightening birds,
seagulls. Look at those eyes

stopped here
forever.
My daughter screamed
as she saw.

Kromsky

On the boat
it is still the same
watching the brown
endless water
like the water in the creek
that stank near the hut
you stopped seeing
the mud the horses
sinking plodding

when you plod
long enough
and people call you
Kromsky the Plodder
just as a joke
there's a kind of love
in the stink the chants
the old men swaying
in the narrow room
forgetting their god

there's a kind of love
in forgetting all words
outside of that room
but love is always
going away as you
had to go
as the ocean goes
toward the island
it is still the same

although everything else
is shifting churning
your stomach is growling
but you're still the same
and the earth spins
in the same direction
and the smells of the crowds
are the smells you know
much too well

and your son clutches
your aching hand
frightened as always
of any stranger—frightened
of anything new
We have traveled for hundreds
of exhausted years
you try to explain
as his eyes swell

but it's still the same
the huge men shouting
their distant words
just like the soldiers
who swept into town
you knew it must
be that way and you ran
home to bed
alive
for one more night

and when your brother appears
magically
out of the crowd
it is still the same
oldest brother with the eyes
you could never meet
and he calls out
in the same voice
Your name is
Levy—a word from some dream
that now
must be yours

The Secret

The children are hiding
in the backyard
telling their secret: Santa is coming
in 2 months—he won't
come if you're bad
he won't come if you throw
your food in the garbage
he won't come if you murder
all your dolls and don't
cure them again
he is coming in a truck
he is coming in a sleigh
with the headlights on—if you lie
awake in the dark
frightened of death
those lights can't shine
if you tell your mother:
I only think the best thoughts
the reindeer will pounce
onto your head
if you hurt your brother
steal a candy speak to the moon
with the wrong voice
Santa's not coming—you have
to be patient you have
to play by the rules
and break the rules
at the right time
know when to ask
for your dearest presents
—pretend not to care
when you don't get them
you must live till you die
still hoping he'll come any minute
to save today—or perhaps he will
save tomorrow
how could it be 1 a.m.
already
much too late

II

Waiting for Night

Railroad Crossing

The wind near the tracks
is too fierce. I've been waiting
for a train to arrive
carrying my parents, my lover,
the dolls I buried close to the house
and couldn't find.
A freight train passes, loaded
with miles of coal.
The black cars rattle,
they will echo for hours.
And the faceless conductor
waves a lantern:
it's getting dark,
it's time to return
to the place you began.
A child whispers into the night:
which is the train
that takes me back?
The lantern just swings.
Her parents watch
from a distant station.
They keep waving
—goodbye goodbye—
as I bend down to caress
the freezing tracks.
This wind has settled
deep in me, its echoes
turned to ice. I have fallen
in love with ghosts.
I can trust them—
they always arrive.

Only Tonight

Cut out the past.
The cool man in the moon was singing
his familiar tune:
There is only tonight,
there is only a circle
with no face, that can't sing.
So I walked on.
The sirens screamed far down
another block—someone was dying.
The moon was a shadow in an empty sky.
The past was a fist pounded so long,
it didn't matter. Someone was dying
in too many distant places.
I read the news
I had read before:
There is no destination and no return.
The moon couldn't stop
being the moon. I couldn't stop
looking up
for something—some clear reason
I walked on.

Gap

I was cold
all last night.
And the words I used
to tell you this
couldn't tell enough, not
how much.

I spoke to you
only in dreams. Your hand
trembled near the rim
of an empty cup—
the appointment was over,
it had been over
months before.
You wanted to get
away. You did

so fast. It's March now,
the wind blows the trees
beginning to bloom
everywhere, almost knocks them
down. But trees survive,
the frantic sky
clears of clouds
and stills. Someone says,
I never thought it could.
That's weeks from now.

Last night
we sat for hours, still
not quite
touching. I dreamed I said

everything
and it didn't matter.
How cold am I?
You ask a child
how much she wants,

she stretches her arms wide,
as wide as they'll go,
and stares at you.
Can't you see?—Just
this much

and more.

Staying Home

It's safe here—
the drills enter only
from nine to five,
some wind barely
cracks my glass,
although last night

it almost did
more. I got through that
shaking. But you see—
I shook for nothing.
My doors remained
locked, the walls held

all they can.
The ghosts who seem
to hate all light
left for good
for now. And I don't believe
in ghosts. I've shut

my blinds
the way a child
shuts her eyes
—tight—
to keep out wind,
the dark that stings

anyway, her parents' voices
saying: you should do
this, that, prepare—
we won't be near
always, something inside
is pulling you

away. That's too
hard to believe.
But they've left
their sterile ghosts
who can't speak
to show—

The Train

A face stares out
past the water,
past the dream
of calm water
she found in a book,
or a life composed
of books, trips
from homes to homes.

She took this trip
as a child, staring
at books, staring
at trees.
          It wasn't the same
and today it is.
The train keeps passing
all her dreams:
she's talking to someone
who drowns in rivers

—the train is too quick—.
She makes him rise
from a river
and talk again.
Their words are unclear.
They see her passing, staring
at no one. And the train
never seems

to move.
          It's a train so
it must be going
somewhere.
She can take the place
she had before.
Inside the train
it's still.

It's Time to Go Home

Where are you going, Mr. Moon?
—Because the child must address
a hard name, a face. A home exists
between the folds of an old book
put away for a lifetime until
the child wakes, if he can, and says,
Where have you gone, dear Mr.?
The moon is hanging alone, not
at any home, and can't speak,
so the child turns back
into someone he doesn't know—the
stranger—the massive *who*?
we drag around.

Parent

The contrived dead stay away
where they belong. They're sad there
and waiting for me to settle the questions
lost to them. But they stay away,
refuse to argue that crucial point
left unsaid, stand in their corner
watching. Last night I turned
the lights on and loud sounds
and pushed them farther away

just to be sure.
I never told you about the hate
I lost, because of time
and watching you: you're caught in a room
crying softly—you can't help it,
you never could. And asked yourself
too little. But that was your life
(the dead are resting
nowhere) and now it's mine.

Running

You can take your bag—home is waiting
in another room, where ghosts will greet you
gently. Your father says:
I've been watching here all night
to iron those foreign creases away,
to hold your head. Your mother will stroke
a child's foot that still shakes:
all those crazy nights are gone
when we punished you for hours.
It was hard to know why. It still is.
It's all gone. The ghosts are
so deeply lost, vaguely held
inside the house. Their room is locked
behind this room. Yesterday
I worked for too many hours, walking through
the empty halls, whispering,
I was meant to leave. Last night you told
it all again: they beat me as a small child
for nothing. I wanted to get far away
from the harm we felt. It was separate
and old. It came to work and came home.
That was yesterday. Put it away
as something strange. Then take it out
in familiar clothes. The past
has always been here. It's us.

A Darkened Road

You've got to use the cold time
you're given. That cold voice
entered mine. It might have been
as a child, trembling through
each night, needing to stay alive
forever: I know there's God,
but where is he, why can't
I feel him?—I felt the night
filled with things that had no name
—they weren't God. Sometimes
my grandmother came to visit me—
her face in the coffin was too white
and too young. They put her in
her wedding dress, the lights in the room
glared. I only looked for one
moment—which is
truly enough. She still comes—
she brings my father, my aunt,
my friends. I can't feel
as much fear, they're too frail.
I used those nights to keep them out, and lost
some hope of night—to let whatever needed me
have me. It's only our world.
It's all our world, but we don't want
all.

******

     God died
just for me, several times,
and will again. But I don't need him
or his death. I walked down
a darkened road. I couldn't see
stars, houses, lights . . .
And trembled through
the lack of signs, proud to be
so brave. There are so many ways
to hold the world away from here.
The cold voice keeps talking:

I know you're still
afraid of night—so choke
on fear and all your ghosts
and open your mouth
wide—

     and beg for more.

Waiting for a Word

The dark tree sings
as if it were

singing. But it's just
a voice like mine

or a voice inside
my belief in trees

—they stand apart
as dark

sinks. In me
alien leaves touch

some branch, try
to caress.

My lover sweeps down
and tightens his grip

and tells some lies
(but they're tender lies).

But we always lie—
what was that truth

I just missed?
The truth is

I can't believe,
I'm in love with

believe

so I listen.

Waiting for Night

Let's go for a walk at sunset.
We'll watch the snow blaze,
burn into night.
I've been waiting for night
to erase the meadow.
When the pictures are lost,
I can close my eyes,
I can vanish far
into sleep—where shattered
friends are waiting.
Their shaking hands reach
across the snow.
I run after one and cry—
leave me alone. He turns,
stares, opens his mouth
and can't speak.
The day my father died
I went for a walk.
The cold leaves crashed
onto the lawn and flared.
His eyes flared. Look—
the sky is flaring. That's it:
we're finished with day.
At last I can curl
into myself
—as the snow keeps glowing,
those hands are reaching . . .
I heard the whispers: he's gone,
leave him alone.
I stroked his hand for hours.
I don't know how to stop.

III

Endings

Endings

This isn't a story of movement,

although we got from home
to here and even
                    beyond.

We found ourselves beyond.
And found it wasn't
ever beyond—the field burned
in front of us, held
by sun, some long hours, I almost screamed . . .

And didn't.
I thought I saved my life.

And found a scream swelling
in. I moved on—the field waved
that day away, the scream became
a part of me

gently.
I told my story: this isn't a story

I ever knew.
             I think
that end and the end comes
and I can't move,
except to gape

at harder ends. I shut
the door and said:
I've learned to shut.
We drove away.

I've learned the scream
by heart, and the way the field might wave
on a cold day, making me
smile. I'm waiting for that. Or just
waiting.

The field knows
a different dance
it might show.

The car might crash,
which won't concern
my story.—It has

an end, sort of:
we've always gotten
somewhere—the paved road twisting
                              wildly—

Make Up Your Mind

I turned to a light
glaring
of myself, always
being made. The appalling day
goes on, unharmed,
no matter how I stare, crush
a withered leaf inside my
chilling hand, and open my hand,
and let the wind take it away, far away, into
nothing. I will be taken, but I have to choose
—right now—this street or the next (where someone
lurks) or the greater fear (where no one lurks
ever, where no one cares). It's the choosing that makes
me. And letting the choice hurt
all over me. I can kill myself. Or find a street,
full, silent, sleeping, for someone
to wake it up.

Or stand here frightened at the crucial thing
I am: I'm dizzy
I'm hiding—

Still There

Staring out, searching—
Or think this
is me: the tracer
of lines so
deeply etched, I didn't know

Or glare
at some eye—to enter
The deep
key of a self:
to need

The self. Therefore I must be

Real.
Repeat it. Or touch the glass to feel
that cold:
flesh meeting—Distinctions
of cold. Still

This hardened pool retains
my sight—is—unmoved
by me (A tear
breaks) No gash, no waves
to prove.

Sunset

There's too much talk—
those soldiers pressed
against the ground
don't care.
Or when they leap
from the ground
to startle friends,
no one says:
I knew you'd come home
sometime. It's either that
or dead. They're going away
tomorrow. The crickets sing
gently: this is the night
to love
night, your heavy legs,
anyone who passes . . .
Some girls pass
knowing—this is the night.
Their dresses dance
like the crickets'
familiar need
and the need of nights
sinking in—. Just to be in
love
with everything

that must sink,
those girls on the ground
staring up

forever.
They left them there.
Don't worry,
the night will speak
for all of us—
every night
its mute breeze chants
goodbye.

Inscription

The plaster broke in my deadened hands
and no one rose
to leave me. And life went on—
remote, exhausted,
unreal. And all that can't be
was.

The angel's wing was
chipped
forever, to be seen as
forever
—a symbol—the pathetic lack
of life.

In the Glass

Fireflies broke
from the dark, startled
us, then lapsed . . .
                    We tried to catch . . .
A wave of dancers fell
out of the wings

—split the stage—

their white gowns died
into the wings
softly. I dreamed you held
yourself in me,
the waltz was slow
and strange. You held yourself
                    away.

The children displayed
life
in glass, the life died,
banging its head
against the glass, trying to find . . .
They never discovered.
That curtain cuts
the audience off, a gentle
thud,
        they're gone.

You whispered something
about your role
(it was too small)
and left. I left
your dream and moved on

as I knew I would.
I survived last night
—it stopped forever—
because I can't believe

forever.
It's in our books:
we need to dream more

                    always . . .

As tonight enfolds
one chilled dream:
there's no
need to believe

            we lapse . . .

Freedom

These blinds cut the room
in strips:

some bars to hold.
Joy is lurking

just outside
or in back of my brain

(where time will stop)
or at the edge

of life—the enticing edge
that is

not. Joy is not
lurking.

That's a fear.
It destroys—

through a day of work,
tapping away

at the typewriter keys
dreaming of a day . . .

through a day
of peace

(it's supposed to be)
when I will drift . . .

The dream drifts on: *It's beyond
my choice.*

The dreamer is still
—a kind of trance:

If only I
had turned

once.—That
horizon keeps blazing

behind.

Where Are You Going?

We can be protected
in the warm room
with the shutters bolted
—winter is rushing

up here in the tree house
we can build a shelter
the bombs are falling

or down
beneath the tree
where the roots hide
where they coil—bind—

Mama said *You came*
from deep inside
I clawed at her stomach

I can be safe
in a lover's arms
for five more minutes
—the alarm keeps ringing
the trucks are crashing
an inch from our door

it is time to take
the blankets away
the broken dolls
the pictures of lovers
who must have died
—I don't hear from them

I hitch
a ride on a truck
perched high above the traffic
the trucker demands
Where are you going?

I am going home
please—hit the gas
hard
take me there quickly
before I notice

I can't arrive

Still Life

The half-rotten apples
are falling already
—which is good
they were meant to fall
the dying were meant
to lose their sight
the tubes are removed
the relatives rush
through the tiny room
collecting things: *This*
was her watch
this was her necklace

the necklace was meant
to survive the wearer
gold it is shiny—it was
cherished for years:
I will hand this down
to my daughter, her daughters
the daughter was meant
to stand at the grave
completely numb:

This is not what I dreamed
and the tears were meant
to startle
the stillest moments
sitting in a garden
staring at apples: they are
fallen, so calm
—a perfect circle

the painter says:
When you realize that life
is a perfect circle
you can almost survive

and she nods her head—just
glaring at
the implacable apples

there seems
nothing else
to do

IV

Mating Time

Broken Away

Those leaves that fell
on the dry lawn
just yesterday
are blown, are scattered—
I have broken away
from another friend
I might have known. For months
his hand will explore
the curve of my hand as I
forget his face,
I try to clutch and he slips
through the dream.
The leaves are drowning
in the shadowed pond
but never drown
completely. The pond is choked
with dead bodies—all
those little deaths
we have to forget.
I have to forget
the way he almost
surrounded me
last night. This morning
dead pictures enclosed
instead of the sun.
The sun has been lost
for five days
as the hope of its brightness
faded, and I thought,
I've felt the last
warmth this year. Already
the winter has bolted
every door.
It's hard to believe
tonight
I'll be dreaming.

Only Air

Take oh take
those arms away
that hurt me in the dark

when they aren't there
the eyes
that don't watch
as I cross the street
caress a leaf

—it is dead already

take the voice away
that refuses to mutter
I love when you bend
to capture those leaves
that can't be caught

I almost felt you
shudder this morning
as I dreamed of death
—diving from a roof
silently
the watch cracked
the time is forever
3 p.m.

and the ones who were loved
almost to the end
cherish that watch
cherish the hour
he climbed the stairs

—did he climb?
looked down at the crowds
—did he bother to look?
thought to himself
—was there any
time to think?
Now I will be
only air

which is too easy
no one can be
only air no one can stop
that figure falling
much too fast—please
take away your body

I can't catch

Meeting

It's a house for the blind
—the perfect symbol—
with your hand almost
crushing the glass,
your eyes almost
touching mine,
then turning down.

I can't see your face.

I never could.
And that's what you loved, a friend said.
I cherished a face that was all my own
—I could make into patterns.
In the dream your hand under the table
entered me,
we talked so little. You said,
Didn't you want to talk?
The blind children ran through the room
stopping my answer.

I have no answer.

I have the answer I don't want.
I need to talk to someone
who has understood—everything
is real in a dream,
it's not like life.
We could sit in a room
for hours, me and the strange
distant you. I would never know who
so desperately

I keep wanting.

Captured

I adhered to my versions
of you:
the thoughts you held
as you stared at the ground,
the way you held me.
We struggled in bed—
two bodies attached
to names. Names, pictures,
the feel of a hand
filled my night . . .
I held my hand.
Outside of me some people
passed,
they were filled with life
(they must have passed).
I couldn't conceive
of them.

They Rush

The birds are excited.
When they mate they rush
from branch to branch
so rapidly, then clash.
We just sit at the cafe table
watching each other, wondering.
Another set of eyes will hide
another world, and I know
I can't press through,
possess that world, belong
to anyone. Those eyes might go
away tomorrow. So we say,
we'll be together forever
—and run to a home
and clutch each other
and try to make
some love.

Shelter

The curtains will protect us
and if not the curtains
the glass doors the storm windows
the blankets we stored
in a distant closet—do you have
the key? place your hand
in my aching hand
we'll be lovers for life
and if not we will fix
the falling roof
that tap where the water
is always cold
—it is freezing this morning
the heater will protect us
did you pay the bill?
did you dream of me as you curled
too tight in the bed—some
terrified child
all the children
keep running to school
or a job or a flight
they must take: I'll be
back tomorrow back
next week or next
year the time will protect us
it is running out

A Slow Goodbye

To make it
less painful, as if pain
were only a tearing

sharply, in the steel wind,
and someone left
behind. I'm unable to go inside

—I don't know where that is.
In the wide apartment
I sit by the phone.

In the silent apartment
I wait by the bed
for the past

to go away
—but always gently.
You came

out of sleep
and pretended to sleep.
You couldn't stand

my open eyes.
When you live away
from clear sight, there is a tear,

a little one.
When you rise from bed
and pass

on the way to doors
—another one.
As you wave: just

goodbye for now, and sit
in the airplane,
on the sofa,

in the park, listening,
and the silence rips
each inch of fabric,

you say—it's better that way,
it must be.
If we just wait,

if we just pretend,
the sound will be
delayed—to save the dear

familiar remnant.
So be careful,
so don't breathe

a few more seconds.

Someone Has Died

Last night you spoke
for hours.
And I couldn't listen.
The clouds were playing
a game with light
—rearranging color.
There were two boys
around the fountain
staring deep
into the fountain.
I wanted to tell them,
I've noticed
treasure inside.
Your father had died
in another dream
and you asked me,
Why?—We can't let them
die for good,
we never stopped dreaming.
I've accepted my father
dying forever.
That's the only father
I have now—
his arms reach out
to clutch, his eyes stare.
And I can't help.
In the other world
the sky turned pink
and deepened.
You didn't look up
as you might
months from now.
I'm watching you
months from now.
When the sky is so living
it's hard to see
your frightened eyes,

your empty hands
trying to clutch
at empty air—
the drowning child
I was.

Mating Time

A crow breaks through
the heavy sky
and all the lost faces
come pouring down
—my lover is dying
a child is crying
Help me I want
to go back to the past
in the arms of a mother
warm dark
with no place to travel—
I have
no place to travel
but I buy all the tickets
drag my luggage
through the long halls
take a train to the south
a train to some country
I have never known
where the frantic lizards drop
from the falling trees
—this is mating time
so I hug myself
and hurry to a meeting
any meeting
with any stranger
the trains are rushing
into the sea—
                never far enough
It's too early for death
the conductor keeps screaming
deep in my ear
—his black
mouth like a crow—he won't
let me sleep

Astonished

When you tried to stare
into my eyes
and hear what I said
when you rolled
over in bed
and clutched me like a child
clutching a doll
when you looked at the picture
in the magazine
and whispered: this
must be you
when you turned and the moon
shot out of your eyes
when you floated in the field
danced on the freezing
bathroom floor
when you stirred the soup and claimed:
this is the best dish I've made
when we stayed up all night
at the typewriter
writing reports—or was it
letters—translations—?
when we spoke the same words
at the same time: *wasn't it isn't it*
how cruel
when I cried all morning
and you never asked:
what could be wrong?
when my aunt died and you paced around
the clotted pond twenty times
and wouldn't come in
when you fell asleep your whole body
dead to my touch
when you cringed at my voice
shouting—really
what could I have shouted?
when you went away

V

Losing the Moon

You Can Live with Stars

       Traveling at the speed of light
the star burned
quietly. I lay on the porch
only for minutes that seemed
for hours and called to the star: just
burn for me, I'm making my wish—
I wish the stars would fall
into my lap, but they always fall
from nowhere to nowhere.
The light I have captured
is nothing of them. My lover said,
the sky is filled with shooting stars,
with meteors you will never see
—at least not here. In the desert the dark
is dark enough, you're free to pretend
you can live with stars and chart their fall.
I saw that light, it covered
the whole desert—my crystal dome
that will shatter, that ends
every dream. He turned away.
I long to destroy what can't be held—
everything
can't be held. He fell asleep, the pale
light still gleamed. I ran to the lawn
and stared at the house and stared at the sky.
We will never meet. But I love to watch us
spinning.

Dancing

Look at the way the flowers shift
as the sudden green enfolds
every petal
at the side of the picture
the green is falling
out of the picture
the flowers are blowing
into a sky they will never reach
they clash forever as if
there were forever
we love to pretend so many things
like: this is a picture
of two flowers
I saw them near the river
as the green surface of river
rose and spun—like a dancer
I said—the painter just turned
this is a picture of the painting
as if he decided
one thing he said I never
can choose a title it's not about
the name

Right Through This

Each morning is vague
as it begins shadowed lights fell
out of the river into my room
a truck marked SANITATION
made too much noise for too little
I couldn't remember why I'm getting up
at this time the alarm kept ringing
I turned it off I won't
try today the drills had begun already
building something it's too
late to stop I drove along the river
two months ago the bridge fell
the cars that streamed along the bridge
and I we all fell into this morning
which is just a light splitting days
from other days I can't leave
loving the drive so much
it stayed with me silently
those noises are hard they know
it's 9 to 5 but the bridge doesn't know
and I don't know deep inside
I never stop and am
drowning right through this it's
morning repeat it it's morning

Air

White sparrows are falling out of the sky
already dead—on the sidewalks I see
hundreds of corpses
and run to the park sweating choking
the dusty leaves are straining
to break from each tree, an old
man is gasping, huddled inside
an enormous coat: it is gray—was it brown
5 years ago? when he started to pace
through the park, one
step at a time, thinking: my life is over
or he's thinking: why is this air
so hard? like little bits of steel
to swallow he must cling to the side of a bench
it is green, the paint chipping peeling
look at those spots of lead on the ground
—he clutches his stomach
the white trucks have arrived
the garbage men spilling out of each door
in their white suits to shovel the birds
throw the remains into some furnace
I can never see—but it churns it growls
tearing the tiny bodies apart
crushing them—the old man keeps staring
—at his shoes? at the dirt?
to see in the dark?
he lifts his head to meet
anyone's eyes—and his eyes are
colorless, as he almost speaks:
Darling, do you know
where I am? Once as a child I had a bird
—a parakeet. I think he was green.
He kept banging his head against the bars
of that dirty cage. But he killed
only himself. They have made it much
too hot out here. I can't breathe.

The Narrator Says

My shadow waits
at the edge of the lawn
and waves to me:
Hello, hello,
but don't come close—

I'll vanish
into you, you'll wonder,
who was there?
The horizon is burning,
the mountains are falling

into night. The narrator says:
It's time to sleep,
nothing has burned,
nothing is lost.
That shadow was always

a part of you.
You approached nothing
that might be held
and opened your arms
—the air was cold.

So I look around.
The narrator was
a part of me, who rushed
across the lawn
and knocked me down.

I lie here staring
at the stars that died
years ago—they still flare—
as the narrator says: Only
their echoes flare

long after. Some things
are hard to stop.

It's the Train Coming

—Back to life I said
because I know the dark
is filled with ghosts
but the narrator answers
that dark only obscures the train
the spotlight shows the same tracks
you ignore at noon
the cars are rusting
they're still sagging
with nothing you know
shipped for reasons that are clear
and safe and hidden
just for now and the haunting
sound is a warning—merely
KEEP OFF THE TRACKS
or be killed as people have been
but we don't talk about that
or the thought that the train
is dying slowly is another
hope from the past that's worn out
and has haunted so many who now
haunt it and I knew I'd return
to the answer I need
a ghost something
with lives of its own
that can go on

No Answers

I dreamed of someone
sitting by the cold sea,
hearing the waves beat
every grain of hard sand
and saying—don't believe
in my dreams, the night beats
inside of you, inside of
no one, it's something we borrow
to live

in our night, the things I said
are your gift too,
if anyone's. The night opened
to swallow him. I needed to shout—
thank you. He shook his head.
I love the way the night sea
drowns

all of us
and dreams of night.
That night I love
everyone. You say that means
no one. It's true—
there's a cold sea
that says

not a thing

but I've heard it
tells   and tells

Ledges

The pale flowers are drifting
  through my window. They'll never fall
    anywhere, and the window is shattered,
      the ledges are drifting. I saw some clouds
        —they had entered within so gently
          the room dissolved. Sometimes I'm almost
            a cloud, all motion, a constant illusion.
              That's just an illusion. Some voices speak
                from the deep woods: you're a stranger here, still
                  outside. So you stack your bricks up and down
                    and pick flowers and place a vase
                      near the window and give words to trees.
                        And you paint a picture: within the picture I am
                          floating—as a flower that's just
                            about to open. And the ledges almost
                              connect, they almost surround, showing
                                it's a picture, it's yearning, it's always
                                  almost—

Losing the Moon

The moon is saying nothing.
I will listen all night.
I will touch the keys
of the shiny piano
and whisper my question—
why do I look?
I look at the moon
for the light it gives
and everything else
I need from sight:
a face, the eyes
that stare back
protecting me
—or they shadow me.
I've been haunted for years
by the full moon
who never was
the friend I dreamed.
The sonata was written
in another time
by a stranger who won't
speak to me.
He stares at the keys
and hears
the moon talking.
Or that's what I thought.
I can't stop thinking.
Look—the room is filled
with distant light.
I lie in bed,
I close my eyes.
And the moon remains
my favorite lover.
His chilled hands reach
deep in me—. I know that is
hard to believe. Every year
the light arrives
from farther away. I rise

towards him, needing
more than his touch.
It's getting late: I want
all the lovers
I will never hold.

Drawn to the Picture

Is it time to go?
She rose and studied the pictures.
She looked at one too hard,
and the narrator said: Here
the people are crossing bridges.
It was time to go, but the painter wouldn't.
The snow froze their toes, their fingers.
Underneath
the crumbling bridge, water was freezing
so hard, you couldn't break through
with a pick, with a razor.
She dreamed of the razor cutting
—a clear cut—as the water streams
and drowns the tourists and drowns the people
drawn to the picture, and the painter
—he closes his eyes. But he dreams,
he keeps dreaming.
The pictures were hidden in books
that lay on her shelf,
dead, so close. The narrator said:
It is time to go
as the painted go: a foot almost
touches the bridge—as she changes the bridge
into something else: the wide
open door, the endless
crossing . . .

Canio's Editions
Literary Paperback Series

Anthony Brandt, *The People Along the Sand*
Edward Butscher, *Child in the House*
Fran Castan, *The Widow's Quilt*
Virginia Christian, Hope Harris, Erika Duncan,
  Three Cautionary Tales
Cyril Christo, *The Twilight Language*
Jane Ciabattari, *Stealing the Fire*
Mark Ciabattari, *Clay Creatures*
Mark Ciabattari, *The Literal Truth: Rizzoli Dreams of Eating
  the Apple of Earthly Delights*
Pat Falk, *In the Shape of a Woman*
Helen Ruth Freeman, *Diurnal Matters*
Dan Giancola, *Powder and Echo*
Jennie Hair, *A Sisterhood of Songs*
William Hathaway, *Sightseer*
Peter Lipman-Wulf, *Period of Internment: Letters and
  Drawings from Les Milles 1939–1940*
Robert Long, *Blue*
Suzanne McNear, *Drought*
Daniel Thomas Moran, *In Praise of August*
Allen Planz, *Dune Heath*
Val Schaffner, *The Astronomer's House*
Davida Singer, *Shelter Island Poems*
Rob Stuart, *Similar to Fire*
Pat Sweeney, *A Thousand Times and Other Poems*
Sandra Vreeland, *The Sky Lotto*
Beverley Wiggins Wells, *Simply Black*

****

For David Ignatow: An Anthology. Among the contributors
are Philip Appleman, Marvin Bell, Siv Cedering, Diana
Chang, Paul Mariani, Joyce Carol Oates, Diane Wakoski.

Kathryn Levy was founding director of The Poetry
Exchange and the New York City Ballet Poetry Project,
two poetry-in-the-schools organizations. She is the
author of *The Nutcracker Teacher Resource Guide*, a guide
to classroom poetry instruction. She has been nominated
for a Pushcart Prize and has received writing fellowships
from Yaddo, the Virginia Center for the Creative Arts, The
Ragdale Foundation, the Blue Mountain Center, the
Vermont Studio Center, and Cummington Community for
the Arts. She has taught poetry to hundreds of public
school students throughout New York City and conducted
courses in literature, film, theater, and arts education for
numerous schools and cultural institutions. She currently
works as a teacher and arts consultant, and divides her
time between Sag Harbor and New York City.